Through Your Own Words
51 Writing Prompts for Healing and Self-Care

Maisha Z. Johnson

Inkblot Arts

Oakland, CA

© Maisha Z. Johnson 2014. All Rights Reserved.

Published by Inkblot Arts
Oakland, CA

ISBN-13: 978-0692349953

ISBN-10: 0692349952

Disclaimer: The information in this book is intended to give readers ideas for writing. It is not intended to substitute for treatment by or the advice and care of a professional healthcare provider.

For survivors everywhere.

Contents

	Page
Introduction	vii
How to Use This Book	viii
Part 1: Through Your Own Words	
Sensations	3
Your Own Words	4
Setting Your Limits	5
Safe Images	6
A Word On Care	7
Welcoming Your Guests	8
Getting Unstuck	9
Every Day	10
Laughter Medicine	11
Taking a Trip	12
Part 2: At Your Own Pace	
Making Meals	15
Your Name's Story	16
One Piece at a Time	17
Your Body's Words	18
I Choose to Feel...	19

Get to Know Your Boundaries	20
Your Own Pace	21
Moving Out	22
Moving In	23
As In...	24

Part 3: In Your Own Place

An Homage to Your Body	27
Chaos	28
Collage	29
Wild Things	30
Art Exhibit of You	31
Inside and Out	32
Set Down a Burden	33
The Room Exercise	34
I've Always Wanted to...	35
Something Bothering You	36
Like Nobody's Watching	37

Part 4: For Your Own Love

Feeling Hope	41
Recipe for Healing	42
How You're Loved	43
Craft Your Umbrella	44
Hunger	45
Letter of Self-Forgiveness	46
Sacred	47

The Tree of Your Thriving	48
Finding Yourself	49
You've Reached a Milestone	50
Part 5: In Celebration of You	
Rest	53
Celebrating Your Survival	54
Boundary Circle	55
Asking for Support	56
Welcome Your Ways	57
Truth	58
Change	59
Your Expert Advice	60
A Letter to Your Future Self	61
Celebration of You	62
Further Reading	
Pieces Quoted in This Book	63
Recommended Reading	65
About the Author and Publisher	66

Introduction

Survivors of trauma are powerful people. We show this every moment as we continue to live and grow in spite of our struggles. What I find most remarkable about our resilience is our creativity, our ability to craft our own sense of what it means to be free. I believe we can foster our own healing just by expressing ourselves, because only we know what's best for ourselves. So I wrote this book as a guide for healing through our own words with writing exercises.

I'm a writer with an MFA in Poetry, and a lifetime of expressing myself through the written word. I'm also a survivor of domestic violence and sexual abuse, and the trauma of those experiences left me with feelings of helplessness and fear. At times, I could express what I was feeling only through my writing.

I see my healing journey as an ongoing process, and I've been fortunate to share space and stories with other resilient survivors along the way. While doing peer advocacy counseling with LGBTQ (lesbian, gay, bisexual, transgender, and queer) survivors of violence through The Trevor Project and Community United Against Violence (CUAV), and facilitating arts and healing workshops with my project Inkblot Arts, I've learned from my communities that we have the power to create the tools we need to survive. Everything we do to stand up for ourselves, from small acts of self-care to courageous acts of storytelling, helps us support ourselves and create the change we need to live fuller, healthier lives.

With this book, I offer my own ideas for claiming written words as one of your tools for healing and self-care.

How to Use This Book

How should you use this book? The easy answer is: however you want. What's most important is your own process, so feel free to get through the writing prompts however you'd like.

You can be a beginning writer or an experienced writer. You can come with your own ideas on how you'd like to write, or go wherever the prompts lead you. I encourage you to follow your own path in your writing, even if it leads you away from the prompt.

I also encourage you to challenge yourself to do all of the prompts, even the ones that don't initially excite you, to see where they lead. You may find a way to write a piece that's closer to your heart. You can do the prompts in order, but you don't have to. If you'd like to read the entire pieces quoted in some of the prompts, you can find sources for them in the chapter "Further Reading" near the end of the book.

Some of the prompts were written with a particular form in mind, like journaling, writing fiction, or writing poetry, but feel free to write in any form you're called to.

Writing for healing and self-care can bring up painful feelings about the trauma we've endured. It can be good to face those feelings, but it's also good to take care of yourself by being aware of your limits. If a topic upsets you, know you can always write about something else or stop writing altogether.

You may find it helpful to create a regular writing practice with these prompts, like doing one prompt a day. Setting aside even as little as ten minutes a day can remind you to prioritize taking care of yourself. And you deserve to take care of yourself. This book is just part of your healing journey, and I hope it can help you find your own words for healing and continue your writing practice long after you've finished working with these prompts.

Your writing is your own safe space to explore the places you go to heal. I wish you well on your journey.

Part 1: Through Your Own Words

1
Sensations

Using the five senses (sight, smell, hearing, touch, taste), describe how you feel right now. What are you touching? What do you see? What, if anything, can you hear? What do you smell? What can you taste? Describe how what you feel with your five senses relates to your emotions. For example: I smell lavender from a candle, and the scent comforts me.

2
Your Own Words

You may have heard many words to describe what you're feeling. Everything from clinical terms to diagnose your ailments to insults like "crazy." It's time to claim your own language for what you've gone through. Come up with a word for how past trauma affects you. You can make it up if you don't find one that fits.

Write a definition of this word, not based on the dictionary, but on your own terms, describing what it means to you. What's the word's origin for you? What does it feel like? How do you know it's present?

Now do the same for the word "heal," finding and defining a word for what healing means to you.

These words are now yours to use in journaling, poetry, and other forms of self-expression. You know their meanings, and you don't have to define them for anyone but yourself.

3
Setting Your Limits

Write down topics you don't want to write about. It can be a simple list, or include detail. Use this however you see fit – as a guide to maintain your boundaries, as an invitation to take on those topics if you find a way that feels safe, or as some combination of the two.

4
Safe Images

Make a list of images that help you feel safe. It can include colors, places, nature, or anything else that comes to mind. Pick one or more from your list and go into detail about what about them helps you feel safe. Try having some of these images around you when you write and see if they change anything about your writing.

5
A Word On Care

Grab a few post-it notes or small scraps of paper. On each one, write a word about what comes to mind when you think of self-care. Spread the words around you and use them as inspiration to write about what self-care means to you and how it helps you survive.

6
Welcoming Your Guests

Be grateful for whoever comes,
because each has been sent
as a guide from beyond.

-from "The Guest House" by Rumi

Rumi's poem "The Guest House" encourages us to welcome all emotions, including the difficult ones, as honored guests. Invite an emotion that comes up for you when things feel hard, and write about it. Where would that emotion stay in your body? What would happen if you invited it to stay? What can this emotion help guide you toward? For example, I might write about how guilt sits in my chest, and examine how guilt guides me toward recognizing when I'm taking on other people's feelings as my own responsibility.

7
Getting Unstuck

Make a list identifying things that make you feel stuck. Pick a few or all of the things from your list and write about how they get you stuck.

Now pick one and write about how you've moved through it in the past, or how you might get through it in the future. Don't be afraid to use your imagination and get outlandish if you're not seeing any reasonable strategies.

For example, if I feel like someone I care about is upset with me, I have a hard time being productive, as I fixate on how they're feeling. One way I've dealt with it in the past is putting on headphones and trying to focus on the music instead of the person's feelings. I can also imagine having a lockbox for setting distracting feelings aside until I have time to deal with them.

8
Every Day

....come celebrate
with me that everyday
something has tried to kill me
and has failed.

-from "won't you celebrate with me" by Lucille Clifton

What's something you struggle with every day, or nearly every day? It can be as simple as finding your keys before you leave the house, or finding time to write as much as you'd like to. Or it can be related to trauma, like avoiding panic attacks or dealing with microaggressions against you.

Describe yourself as a warrior facing this challenge, and celebrate your daily victories.

9
Laughter Medicine

What makes you laugh? Find something simple and easily accessible - an online video, a funny passage in a book, a memory of a good time with a friend - and let it make you laugh. Feel how the laughter moves through your body, and write about what joy feels like to you.

10
Taking a Trip

i say i'm on the path to healing,
as if healing is a city i'll reach someday,
on a street corner shimmering in stardust
just past the intersection of lasting scars
and stitched-up smiles—
a place so real,
i'll sear my lips with an asphalt kiss when i get there.

-from "healing" by Maisha Z. Johnson

Imagine your healing journey as an actual expedition. What would you take with you on your trip? How would you pack? How would you travel - at what speed, and by what mode?

Write about preparing for and embarking on your healing journey.

Part 2: At Your Own Pace

11
Making Meals

Write about what keeps you going as if these things were meals. Come up with your own terms for what each meal represents for you, or use the following guide.

What is your breakfast made of? What wakes you up, welcomes you to the day, and gives you fuel to sustain yourself?

What is your lunch made of? What helps you feel permission to pause in the middle of life, to re-energize for the rest of your journey, to keep moving when you begin to feel depleted?

What is your dinner made of? What comforts you as you calm down, helps you come back to yourself after exerting your energy?

If you want, you can also include your snacks, which add a spark to your life throughout your journey, and your desserts, the rewards you give yourself not only for nourishment, but for sweetness, too.

12
Your Name's Story

In English my name means hope. In Spanish it means too many letters. It means sadness, it means waiting. It is like the number nine. A muddy color. It is the Mexican records my father plays on Sunday mornings when he is shaving, songs like sobbing.

-from *The House on Mango Street* by Sandra Cisneros

What's the story of your name? What does it mean? Where did it come from?

Our names can have different meanings depending on who we are. Write about what your name means to you. What words can describe you, and therefore define your name? What defining moments have contributed to the meaning of your name? You can do this with your given name, a nickname, or a name of your choosing.

13
One Piece at a Time

When you think about the source of your trauma, it can be overwhelming to share about everything that happened all at once. You don't have to tell it all. Pick just one part, starting with something that feels small. I might choose the socks I was wearing or what I ate at the beginning of that day. Write about that small part, even if writing the details takes you away from the traumatic event in your life.

You can come back to this and write one small piece at a time, and stop at any point.

14
Your Body's Words

Close your eyes and squeeze your muscles one by one as you are able, from your toes up to your forehead. See what you notice about how the parts of your body work together. Imagine your whole body in conversation, each part speaking to the others to help keep you alive. Now record the conversation, writing down how the parts of your body communicate.

15
I Choose to Feel...

We can't always choose our emotions, but imagine for a moment that you can. What would you choose to feel right now? Joy? Relief? Comfort? Write "I chose to feel..." and describe the emotion, what thoughts and images it brings up, and how it feels in your body. See where making this choice would lead.

16
Get to Know Your Boundaries

Get to know your boundaries by writing about how you feel in your body. Close your eyes, and bring your attention to your skin. Where do you like to be touched? Where do you prefer not to be touched? Which parts of your body are you more comfortable exposing, or more comfortable covering up? Then bring your attention to the space around you. Where do you exist beyond the borders of your skin? How close or far do you prefer others to be?

Write what came to your mind during this awareness exercise. Then continue on to list your boundaries. Feel each one in your body and describe how it keeps you safe.

17
Your Own Pace

"I'm going back to bed."

Your healing is all about you, but oftentimes we think about "getting over" what we've been through in terms of the outside world. We feel the pressure to heal in order to function, to go to work, to take care of other people.

For a moment, think of your healing as impacting only your sense of a healthy self, and nothing else. What pace would you find if it were all your own choosing? What choices would you make to slow down or change priorities?

Chart your dream healing journey, thinking about what choices you would make just for you, and how those choices would take care of you.

18
Moving Out

I choose to take this anger you've left in me. It gives me strength.

Imagine you're moving out of the building that houses your trauma. What would you take with you, if anything? How would you leave things behind - just as they are, or in boxes? Or would you burn it all before you left?

Using the metaphor of moving out of the building that houses your trauma, describe your process of moving on.

19
Moving In

Imagine moving into a place of healing as finding a new place to live. Write about this healing place. What about it helps you heal? The colors? The outside setting? Describe your process of moving in. What do you unpack first? Do you settle in all at once, or over time? How do you know this healing home is yours to keep?

20
As In...

queer as in no parts
fit quite perfectly with mine.
no body parts
or parts of the globe
or parts of speech
in this language we speak.

-from "what do i mean by queer?" by Maisha Z. Johnson

Pick a part of your identity that's important to who you are. Perhaps it's your gender, your nationality, your calling. Using the refrain "_____ as in _____" or your own sentence structure, write about what that identity means to you, regardless of how others may define it.

Part 3: In Your Own Place

21
An Homage To Your Body

..these hips
are free hips...

-from "homage to my hips" by Lucille Clifton

In the spirit of Lucille Clifton's "homage to my hips," praise a part of your body. How has your body helped you survive?

22
Chaos

How do you feel about chaos? How does the word sound on your tongue, and feel in your body?

Write a before, during, and after account of being in chaos.

23
Collage

Collect words, phrases, and sentences that resonate with you. You can search books, poems, magazines, and choose images if those resonate, too. Put them all together in random order or however they make sense to you. If they are printed, you can spread them out on the floor or a table.

Take a look at them all together, and see what they have to say. Does grouping them change their meanings? Find links between them and use the connections to write a new piece, with the words you've collected and your own. You can write multiple pieces across multiple connections, or try to write one piece that fits them all.

24
Wild Things

...For a time
I rest in the grace of the world, and am free.

-from "The Peace of Wild Things" by Wendell Berry

If you were among wild things, where would your place be? Write about what you would be if you were part of nature. An animal? A plant? An element like earth, water, air, or fire? What would be your role as this wild thing, and what would that role mean to you?

25
Art Exhibit of You

There's a new art exhibit on display, and it's all about you! Write about attending the opening of the exhibit. Who would attend? Are there people you'd want to have there for support? People you'd want to face the pain they've caused you? Or would you want to be alone with the art? Walk through the gallery and describe what you see. How is your personality portrayed? Your body? Moments in your life?

Take your time writing about this exhibit, because there may be many things to see, and as with all art, each piece may hold many possible meanings. With each pass, you might notice something you didn't see before.

Pay particular attention to the pieces that honor your strengths. None of the other pieces would be possible without those.

26
Inside and Out

Describe your outer self, how you present yourself to the world. Then describe your inner self, how you feel inside. Write about the ways they're different, and the same.

Then describe the process of your inner and outer selves coming together as one. How would they reconcile their differences? What would you choose to keep from the outside, to help yourself feel safe? What would you fiercely hold onto from the inside, knowing it must be a part of you? How would you feel in the fullness of your whole being? Would you still have differences between your outward presentation and your inner self? Remember no answers are right or wrong.

27
Set Down a Burden

Sometimes we strain under the weight of burdens we don't even know we're carrying. Imagine setting down a burden. Where do imagine releasing tension from? Your hands? Your shoulders? Your chest? Give the burden a shape, a size, a color, a weight. Describe it and examine it. What is it made of? Where did it come from?

28
The Room Exercise

You do not have to be good.
You do not have to walk on your knees
for a hundred miles through the desert repenting.
You only have to let the soft animal of your body
love what it loves.

-from "Wild Geese" by Mary Oliver

Read the poem "Wild Geese" by Mary Oliver, or if you can't access it, just reflect on the passage above. Create a room in which you don't have to be good. It can be an actual room, or a house, a place in nature, or another image that comes to you. This is a place where you can go to connect with yourself, in your nature, apart from any outside expectations or obligations. Write about the details of this place - what does it look like there? What can you see, hear, and smell? If you want, add something imperfect to this place. Perhaps you run your fingers down cracks in the paint.

Keep this place in mind to return to when you need to.

29
I've Always Wanted To...

Think of something you've always wanted to do, but haven't done. What's holding you back? Write about why you'd like to do it, and why you haven't yet.

Now think about what it would mean for you to do this. Pick a first step toward doing what you've wanted to do, and write about what it would be like for you to take that first step, and any steps you can imagine coming after it.

Feel free to go wherever this piece leads you - it may even lead you to taking a first step!

30
Something Bothering You

Write about something that's been bothering you lately.

Now think of a moment when it wasn't bothering you - maybe you were distracted, focused on a task, or in a good mood. Write about what allowed you to take your mind away from what's been bothering you.

31
Like Nobody's Watching

Do a silly dance. However you are able, and with whatever you need to get you moving - put on some music if you want, close the blinds if you have to. Move not how you think you should be moving, but how your body feels like moving. Let your sense of joy be your guide.

Now write about how it felt to move like that. What happened in your body? What hesitations did you feel? How do you give yourself permission to move freely?

Part 4: For Your Own Love

32
Feeling Hope

What gives you hope? Write a list of things, no matter how big or small. Then dive into one at a time, detailing its meaning and impact on you.

33
Recipe for Healing

Ingredients:
1 outdoor park
70 degree F weather
1 book of poems by Gwendolyn Brooks
3 friendly dogs (not my own, so I can play with them but I don't have to clean up their poop)
3 hours of free time

Instructions: Apply three hours of free time to the outdoor park. Add book of poems by Gwendolyn Brooks, and allow time to read each poem slowly while taking deep breaths, and to feel the words in my bones. Allow interruptions only for dogs to visit, resting their heads on my lap and letting me rub their heads.

Write a recipe for your healing. It could be for one night of self-care, a morning grounding routine, or any process that would feel restorative for you. List the ingredients, then the instructions for application. While you write, take on the role of head chef, remembering that you have all the expertise you need for what feels good to you. Keep coming back to this recipe, or create a whole book of recipes for when you or someone in your life wants to know more about your needs.

34
How You're Loved

Think about someone who loves you. Write about what you mean to them. Use exaggeration and gush wildly if it helps you come up with the words. What about you makes you loveable?

35
Craft Your Umbrella

Umbrellas are designed to keep us dry when it's raining. If you could carry something over your head to protect you, what would it be made of? Your favorite color? Comforting words? Craft your umbrella, then describe the materials and what it protects you from. What dangers come at you throughout the day, and how do you keep them away? You can imagine carrying this umbrella with you wherever you go, in case of rain.

For a bonus activity, use paper, images, and words to make a little umbrella to symbolize your protection.

36
Hunger

and he said: you pretty full of yourself ain't chu

*so she replied: show me someone not full of herself
    and i'll show you a hungry person*

-from "Poem For A Lady Whose Voice I Like" by Nikki Giovanni

What are you hungry for? Write about it, see it before you, and feast.

37
Letter of Self-Forgiveness

Part 1: Think about all the things you haven't forgiven yourself for. Write a letter of apology to yourself, asking for forgiveness, explaining what you did and why - what led you to making the choice you made. You may get stuck on some things, because chances are, some of the things you hold against yourself aren't wrongdoings, or they're not your own wrongdoings to take responsibility for. If you come across something that you don't need to apologize for, write that down and set it aside. You may not need to apologize for any of the things that come to mind.

Part 2: Write a letter of forgiveness to yourself. If the choice you made was understandable under the circumstances, say that. If you know you were just doing what you had to do to survive, say that. If it's hard to forget but you can work on forgiveness, say that. And if something you did was not your wrongdoing, write it out to let yourself know, so you can begin to let it go.

38
Sacred

sa·cred *adjective \ˈsā-krəd\: highly valued and important : deserving great respect*

-Merriam-Webster Dictionary

What do you hold sacred? Write about what's sacred to you..

39
The Tree of Your Thriving

Use paper and scissors to cut out parts of a tree - roots, pieces of the trunk, and something to bloom, like flowers, fruit, or leaves.

On each root, write or draw a representation of a word that describes what grounds you, something you know is always a part of you, even if others don't always see it. For example, a root of mine would be faith, which I don't always explain to other people, but I know is always with me, keeping me strong.

On each piece of the trunk, write or draw a representation of something that's always a part of how you show up in the world, perhaps in terms of how you treat other people or yourself. For example, a piece of my trunk would say "compassion."

On each bloom, write or draw a representation of a word for what gives your life an extra spark of energy, adding joy and flair. For example, one of my blooms would be creativity.

Now craft your tree by putting it together from root to trunk to bloom. Using these words, write about the tree of your life, or how you thrive.

40
Finding Yourself

The term "finding yourself" is often used figuratively, as in becoming and accepting the person you want to be. Here's a chance to experience this viscerally. Write about walking through a desert (or someplace else you'd like to wander) and coming across your fullest, truest self. What do you see? What do you think the self you find would say? What would you want to ask yourself about the freedom to be your true self? What would the two of you have in common?

41
You've Reached a Milestone

Think of a milestone you'd like to reach in your healing process, and write as if you've reached it. For example: "I don't have nightmares anymore." How do you feel after reaching this milestone? What's different about your life? What have you preserved? How did you accomplish this?

In your writing, honor at least one way you're already moving in the direction of this milestone. For example, I might write about the ways I've learned to breathe deeply to help me relax before sleep.

Part 5: In Celebration of You

42
Rest

What does rest mean to you? Write about what it means and how it feels. Use your five senses to imagine every detail about what the word "rest" brings to your mind.

43
Celebrating Your Survival

Tell the story of something that's caused you pain, through the lens of celebrating how you survived. For every choice you made, describe the details of how that choice took care of you at the time. How would this story end if it's written in celebration of your survival? Give this piece the conclusion it deserves, a summary of how your wise choices have taken care of you.

44
Boundary Circle

On a piece of paper, draw a circle. On the outside of the circle, write what you're saying "no" to when you're setting boundaries. For example, are you saying no to unsafe spaces? To touching without your consent? Inside the circle, write what you're saying "yes" to by setting those boundaries. To getting enough rest? To love that feels good to you?

Take a look at your YESes and NOs. What kind of life says yes and no to these things? Write about what your Boundary Circle says about the kind of life you're living with the boundaries you have.

45
Asking for Support

If you could ask for help with your healing, what would you ask for? Allow yourself the freedom to think about what you'd really want to ask for, regardless of any self-consciousness about your needs or hesitations about what you feel is possible to ask for.

Write either an open letter or a letter to someone specific, asking for support. Detail what you'd need and how, without using justifications or apologies.

Then write a thank you letter to yourself, sharing your gratitude for speaking up for your needs.

46
Welcome Your Ways

Oftentimes we see the aftereffects of trauma in a negative light, feeling like the ways we move through the world are all wrong. Write a list of your coping skills, and include the ones you may think of negatively. For example, I may include something I think of as good, like writing, and something I tend to judge myself for, like feeling numb when I don't want to deal with a difficult emotion.

Now, since all of your coping skills have entered your life at some point, write a welcome to them, recognizing their good intention of coming to you to keep you safe. For any skills you no longer find useful, you can thank them for their time with you and start to say good-bye.

47
Truth

And if sun comes
How shall we greet him?
Shall we not dread him,
Shall we not fear him
After so lengthy a
Session with shade?

-from "truth" by Gwendolyn Brooks

Sometimes our truth is hard to face, and yet at the same time, it nourishes us to stand in the light of our truth, rather than hiding in fear and shame. Think of a part of your truth that fits this description. Perhaps it's the truth of who hurt you, and how. Perhaps it's the conditions we live in to allow violence to happen.

Write about your truth and how it nourishes you to bring it to light, even if this truth is for your eyes only.

For example, when I move away from blaming myself for my own sexual assault, I notice the external forces that let sexual assault go unnoticed. And for me, those outside forces are even scarier than feeling like there was something I should've done differently to keep the attack from happening. But acknowledging rape culture as truth gives me the tools to face it and help create a different reality.

48
Change

Think about a way that you've changed. It can be a small change, like adding new colors to your wardrobe. Or it can be as significant as gaining more language to talk about your trauma. Create a road map of that change. See if you can chart the gradual shift, or a major turning point. For each point on the map, record the differences in how you felt and showed up in the world.

Write an account of how you changed and what you were moving toward with that change. You can use this process with multiple changes to recognize that you are changing in some ways, no matter how small. You may have a ways to go, but you've started the process. What does that mean for you?

49
Your Expert Advice

You've just received a letter from your past self. You wrote it just after a painful moment, asking for advice on how to survive. And since your current self is the only person who knows first-hand what your past self has gone through, you're the expert on how best to get through this.

Write a letter to your past self, and tell them how you've healed. Use the expertise you've gained through experience to advise your past self on how to take care of yourself so you can survive through today and beyond.

50
A Letter to Your Future Self

Think of a point in the future when you imagine you might like to hear from yourself now - it could be six months, a year, twenty years from now. Write a letter to your future self. Tell yourself what you're doing now to survive and heal, and remind yourself of what you know about your needs. Tell yourself about the long-term needs you're addressing today to get yourself into the future. Remind yourself to feel proud of all you've done.

51
Celebration of You

It's time for a celebration of you, of all that you are, have been, and will be. Write about how this celebration would look. Would it be a big, grand party? A small gathering? A solitary moment? What about you would you want to celebrate? It can be anything from your fabulous hair to your kindness to your survival. How would you want to be celebrated? Would your guests give glowing toasts, create art in your honor, or give you the gift of the alone time you crave? Spare no detail in describing this celebration of you.

Further Reading

Pieces Quoted in this Book

Part 1

Welcoming Guests
Rumi. "The Guest House." All Poetry. Web.
 http://allpoetry.com/poem/8534703-The-Guest-House-by-Mewlana-Jalaluddin-Rumi

Every Day
Clifton, Lucille. "won't you celebrate with me." Poetry Foundation. Web.

http://www.poetryfoundation.org/learning/guide/237892#poem

Taking a Trip
Johnson, Maisha Z. "healing." Fierce Hunger: Writing from the Intersection of Trauma and Desire. Ed. Jen Cross. 2013. Print.

Part 2

Your Name's Story
Cisneros, Sandra. "Names" from The House on Mango Street. New York: Vintage Books, 1984. Web. The Literary Link.
 http://theliterarylink.com/mangostreet.html

As In...
Johnson, Maisha Z. "what do i mean by queer?" Queer As In. Oakland, CA: Inkblot Arts, 2014. Print.

Part 3

An Homage to Your Body
Clifton, Lucille. "homage to my hips." Poetry Foundation. Web.
  http://www.poetryfoundation.org/poem/179615

Wild Things
Berry, Wendell. "The Peace of Wild Things." Poetry Foundation. Web.
  http://www.poetryfoundation.org/poem/171140

The Room Exercise
Oliver, Mary. "Wild Geese." University of New Mexico. Web.

http://www.phys.unm.edu/~tw/fas/yits/archive/oliver_wildgeese.html

Part 5

Hunger
Giovanni, Nikki. "Poem for a Lady Whose Voice I Like." Poetry Foundation. Web.
  http://www.poetryfoundation.org/poem/177835

Truth
Brooks, Gwendolyn. "truth." Poetry Foundation. Web.
http://www.poetryfoundation.org/poem/242240

Recommended Reading

Writing Down the Bones by Natalie Goldberg

The Artist's Way by Julia Cameron

Writing Ourselves Whole by Jen Cross
 http://writingourselveswhole.org

About

Maisha Z. Johnson is a writer and creative facilitator living in Oakland, CA. Through writing and arts and healing workshops, she lifts up voices of those who are often silenced, including LGBTQ people, people of color, and survivors of violence. Maisha is the author of three chapbooks, *Queer As In* (Inkblot Arts 2014), *Uprooted* (Gorilla Press 2014), and *Split Ears* (Aggregate Space 2014), and a first full-length poetry collection, *No Parachutes to Carry Me Home* (Punk Hostage Press 2015). Maisha studied creative writing at San Francisco State University and earned her MFA in Poetry from Pacific University. Her work has been published in numerous journals and nominated twice for a Pushcart Prize. She has been a featured reader at literary events and social justice rallies throughout the Bay Area, and she blogs about the relationship between writing and social change.

Inkblot Arts is an Oakland-based project to amplify voices through writing, arts, and creative facilitation. Inkblot Arts includes editing services and healing arts workshops to cultivate creative self-expression and community empowerment.

www.inkblotarts.org

www.ingramcontent.com/pod-product-compliance
Lightning Source LLC
Chambersburg PA
CBHW061340040426
42444CB00011B/3017